A BOOK

A BOOK

A PAGE

YOUCAXTON PUBLICATIONS

OXFORD & SHREWSBURY

00358

saturday night in the pub
a wonderful sunday roast
queuing for the bus
after tea and toast
trying to find a seat
on the early morning train
and watching the farmer
exposing himself
along a country lane

00371

the senses were laughing
at the fact that
Immanuel Kant
but the watering can
so much so
they lost
the frequency
and the idea that the
daft old fool
still thought
that living your life
as if every act were
to become a universal law
maintained the giggles
late into the evening

00381

take me away
for a year and a day
to live with joy
at its best
then
take me away
for an hour and a day
to lie beside
at its rest
then
take me away
for a minute and a day
to kiss with you
at its lest

00385

during dinner
the compulsion
to thrust
my knife
into my chest
is only prevented
by a vision
that one day
I will be fed
stew on
a silver spoon
by a free spirit
with the breath
and breeze
of Aine

00386

neither milk warm
nor frostbitten frames
bring sill to the life
when sleep mourns
stifled light dusts
all things to shade
and soft stone pillows
nestle with mosses
the clover lawns pain
as summer wasps to a death
forsaken plants bow
until the never ending leaves

00420

I adore the word
petunia
for it doesn't rhyme with
violence
I also adore
silence
and that does

00423

I affectionately reach
into my stomach
to pull out my intestines
and neatly
place all twenty five feet
around the chair for good measure
I can now comfortably reach up into
my chest cavity
it takes my breath away
and I give my lungs a little nudge
for old time sake
then I manage to extract
my beating heart
It's a quick but onerous task
as I place it neatly
on the table
adjacent to the condiments

00424

life under a stone
is a heavy burden
but where do you go from here
will they take me away
to subsist with the rest?

00427

from daubed walls
and hedgerows
sparrows slip into the skull
through the eye socket
for a covetous rest

just another retreat
I've owned
and never lived in

00428

you rolled them over

so much bigger and sweeter
than anything they
had ever tasted

then crushed them
there and then

yet

you roll away from me
smaller
than a stick of pink rock
with cunt written through it

00432

accelerating ice cold
droplets of water
drip down the back of my collar
from the cracked guttering

it's now almost clear enough to see
the grey rainbow of intellect
and it's heralded
pot of capacity

I'd like to move closer
but I've waited almost four hours
on this spot
for this exhilarating thaw

00435

I found and met a being
too beautiful for me
this being held a darkness
that taught me to be free
this darkness was a lesson
the best I've ever had
the beauty never faded
and this always
leaves me sad

00437

home was where
the plate was wiped with bread
happiness was where
the ball was kicked till noon
love was where
where ever mother was
and joy was
where the sun lies down
before the harvest moon

00440

my silence wails
a naked truth
against the stones

a baleful wind
blows yew berries
into four equal mounds
unto the corners of a plot

my fortune my finale

00447

a worn wedding ring
worn to the bone
a measure of life
now sits alone
the ups and downs
of the stories it tells
begins and ends
with the ringing of bells

00451

the genius in the bottle
slowly drowns with dirt under
his nails
the dog-rose
has torn a vein
and this fusion creates a
dissipation of the soul
in turn
this produces a scent
that
causes grown men
to tear flesh from bone

00456

you arranged cutlery
symmetrically almighty
as love ran amok
gouged out an eye
and bled eternal tears
stridently pacing
with the door ajar
your rancour
strewn on their bed
as we suckled

00459

it's been nine days
finally
nails tap on wood
afore
seeping
hooded eyes lour
from
a distorting black abundance
some
clutch at spiders
others
expires them
down my brittle throat

00463

he was a masterpiece
with a big pinch of salt
and regulated by mealtimes

he'd tear off both your ears
under his order of silence

which was a small price to pay
for the subtlety
of a pot of darjeeling
and two custard creams

00467

the person in the hallway
is no longer moving
it's been two hours
and thirty-six minutes

during this time
a watch
ten nails
hair
and
thirty-one teeth
have been posted
on to the doorstep

00472

crossing an English bridge
I know I'm almost there
above the dark Welsh waters
where Sabrina drowns a prayer
the medieval groping lanes
of a Salopian town of flowers
where Darwin evolved in origin
and I've drank my finest hours

00475

rambling with solitude
with a desperate desire
to own nothing but my mind

to be free to think
free to roam
free to call this world my home

with no allegiance
to gods nor beasts

00476

carrying the kingdoms key
we trod a sacred path
below the spirits of the Clans
we drained the midday wrath

cooling hearts and bones
in a palmed shaded dune
we drowned a sear thirst
before a hilal moon

our ascendancy to nature
ran along the perishing creeks
where we closed our minds, and listened
to the Arabian wind that speaks

then the essence of our wilderness
doused us with a light
as we dreamt with constellation
that embraced the desert night

00501

so far away
from the day
for no reason
nor season
just flat
that's that
but like the prune stone
It will pass

00503

I missed the boat
but still afloat
to tell the tale
of no avail
to those who stared
but rarely cared
I hid
at least I thought I did
I embraced the light
to endure the night
to understand
this abject land
to my favourite friends
this never ends
If you wonder why
I could always fly

00505

I'm moving on
no slow balloon
to lie under blooms
to take light
from the moon
love too left the rooms
in the blink of an eye
I'm under a stone
with gristle and bone
saying hello to good bye

00507

paddling in purgatory
below seabirds
she hauled her carcass
and temple of concern
through hedges

while grappling
with her stunning spirit
every second of every stare
to bring me diction
and riches greater than god

I paid lip service in quiet tones
and witnessed her graceful world
from a cobweb

00510

greasy love spoon

epileptic fits
on tattooed tits
and my musical hall
sings for its supper

where psychedelic wines
from the treacle mines
are just a stone's throw away
from this cuppa

with transient fats
under porkpie hats
balanced on top of the stall

where the hugging of trees
and the birds and the bees
really amount to
fuck all

00514

the Bard made him hard
in a messy regard
and he's feeling king Lear
from the ploughman's and beer
take him to the rose garden
while I cosy the tea pot
for his visions of England
Horatio Isambard Jethro
wherefore art thou?

00516

this way up

the wheelchair deflated the sand
no fabled miracle
as raw working anger
spilt buckets of bile

an amateur crawl
over a million shitty pebbles

no mop required

for this 'kick in the balls' spastic fling

just tell them

'for your tomorrow I swam today'

00517

are we naive
are we the same
are we happy
are we playing the game
ordinary people leading ordinary lives
ordinary husbands, ordinary wives
letting wedlock slip through their hands
simply because love understands
some face the truth
some live a lie
some make it work
some don't even try

00527

the skeletal one bleeds
as the fat one pleads
not to go out in the city
there's a cellar to sweep
where we both can sleep
and not have to tolerate pity
hunger chants
and rips off its pants
and chases the fat one away
then reticence screams
to wake from these dreams
and diet the rest of the day

00528

as I sat with myself
fifty years apart

this young child
looked up at me

we so love one another

but not ourselves

00529

If I leave my cream tea cold
by my
or god's frail hand
tell them
of the price of love
in our unpleasant land

'skipped with the rope'

00533

a flashback of the fairytale
shakes me
to where she drew me hither
to inherit my mind

my valentine
my dais queen

raise me
raiseth upon me
fly me as the supine kite
to keep me
in this delicious place forever

my valentine
my dais queen

your gentle steppingstones
are far and wide
and I am weak for a strong heart
that speaks

00544

It was an open opportunity for tea
and a one-way conversation
within the secret life of curtains
she was a strange shade of silence
curvy turbulently blessed
and the owner of a heavy storm

I briefly forgot about life and humility
and life forgot to escape with a smile
but the fear of God was everywhere
and she prayed hard
that I was a father
but no teeth could bare
that amount of sweetness
and when they built the road on the show
I died of thirst

00545

my mind seeks hiding places
from the ghosts of solace
as the spider and I
keep tabs on the sky

new winds take hold
ornate with cold
and smiling from on high

as the clouds bear illusions
of spineless collusions
I'm teaching this spider fly

so lock up your dreams
for it's all that it seems
now that only the living can die

00553

beyond the eyes
lies a cemetery of pain
where yesterday's contradictions
brought dead flowers once again

branded within deaths domain
with an ignorance of belief
the ties of love and longing
weave the binding for the grief

so happy birthday dead person
I hope your enjoying this show
but there's very little left of me
just the usual to and fro

00556

the creaking
body woes

the tormented
mind goes

tick tock tick tock

from a lifetime of following
an imaginary clock

00561

four walls
three holes
two balls
ones goals

00567

striving to be someone
you're not
to go
somewhere
you don't need to be
flaunts
then
taunts
then
haunts
as you slowly neglect being free

00568

the realm of the ancestral pocket watch dreams
when our red line
saw the whites of their eyes
and the fog of war
filled the empires skies
for only England does what English do

00571

as a soul
I walked through the gate
and crossed the line
to redefine hate
I ate sandwiches in Dante's hell
where lust pride and avarice
would wait for the bell
and as I sat with the damned
I knotted a rope
my subject was sin
and I abandoned all hope

00573

within the variants of blue and black
where toys are reinforced
the destructive nature of man
deals another hand
the gold stars of venus
are no longer of consequence
now that the semi permeable membrane
is porous
so simply cancel the direct debits
and our great civilisations collapse

00574

beneath the history of clouds
a big fork feeds
the renaissance
of garish thoughts
with garrulous words
and the bigger the words
the better the barley mow

thus a water mill of tears
flood the homes
that we've never owned

while a cocktail of cabinets
swill our ears with
the relevance of sincerity

and as protégés
we tolerate the arsonists
pouring petrol on the anarchists

00575

beautiful waiting room

boats on the shoreline
wait on latent dreams
for that high tide

there is now blood in his shit!

and this architecture
simply accentuates insignificance

00576

the sun is crooked today

a sanitised sunrise
brings fresh food to the table

this is now our home children

00577

a man of few words

not a man of war
not a man of god

normal be
normal die

00580

the distance to tomorrow has lapsed
and the cartographer's drugs
are on the line

there is a spotless vibrancy
where the carrots taste like pineapples
and the motels smell of neon

she's busy biting my fingernails
and waving a short straw
at anyone who'll clean her glasses

but the new furrows in her brow
could grow carrots or pineapples

and so the story begins

00581

this is your hell
these are my centuries

what comes natural is unnatural

not we equal are
and
ten millennia
of gods soldiers fairies and science

fucking hallelujah

00583

I quietly coloured in a world
then my feet were measured
where the memories had the crusts cut off
silently my mind set with the blancmange
so I no longer craved dessert
then as I was taken from behind
I had saccharine and thyme on my mind
but the orgasm during the rape
was always omitted from the tape
seen and not heard
has never spoken
and all bad machines
are forever broken
and thankfully the kindest disposition
lead to this favourable position

00584

a cheese cloth shirt
without a bra
and her sticky fingers
are back in the jar
it took me twenty minutes
to lick away
twenty years of honey

00585

sadness flourished
before my curt bow
as all bar one
replied in the past tense
the coroner was so aroused
that the judge demanded a blindfold
and all before a jury
that sat like a month of sundays
slowly stirred into a thick bucket of shit
perjury ran amok for days
within an oganised frenzy
of sweaty hand on sweaty gland
thankfully my torture blinds like new pencils
having written
just one small word in the future tense

00586

more icicle than bicycle
she wrung necks
to the sound of dogs barking
then cried for what she is not
before a village that never forgot

her famed unreceptive touch
held a deceptive
once in a lifetime crutch
but now her feet are free
from vales that pale from grey

now burghers greet by screaming
in one another's faces
on babbling brook bridge of all places
I do hope she smiled between gates
and found the sisters kiss

00587

Puck is not drinking the milk
and the thumbed copy
of the beginner's guide to sinners
keeps the voyeur's door ajar
so that
the expansive mind
as you will find
can always dance for Degas
and there is always a use for spilled milk

00588

as the shepard
I walk the same

until I walk into darkness
until I wake in light

I wake the same
as the shepard

00589

she was on all fours
in an excavation
and even she has no explanation
as to why the finishing and starting line
are simply drying my clothes
but these things have a depth
of martyrdom
so always mind your speak

00590

they married an affair
without a care
in this sacred land
where control and sexual gratification
go hand in hand

her dress of no return
complements the crooked aisles
and as new blood fills the phallus
the last artisan beguiles

held down by fiends
with wild contortions
in this domain
they create
the most beautiful abortions

00592

the yellow bird is up in the banana tree
staining care
with menstrual wine
as a tortured treasure
most of this time
with arms in knots
fragrant forget me nots
linger on and on and on
slurring upon a dozen steps
like waves
where the futile apostles
shaking like mongrels
shit three rusty nails

00593

the joy of touch
fights with the joy of taste
as the moon bids farewell
I find my mind
breastfeeding paupers
as the blur of poverty
scatters all cushions
while defecating decadence
the usual victims are rubbing brass
while raiding tombs
from panic rooms
without a weekend pass
thus ordinary greed
make extraordinary gestures
when the gift lies hidden

00595

fear has knocked hope clean out
and feasting on femininity
is now lodged behind the blindfold
that complements the scold's bridle
rolling pins
cake tins
napkins
but come morning come dawning
the exploration of veridical men
will punish this cowardly new world
with a reinvention of war

00598

the old man with the spoon
said he's going soon
the doctors told him June
as they really need the room

00600

Dearest meal

the exhaustive pranks
of think tanks
and food banks
reinforce that I own nothing but time

yours sincerely

four walls
and no missed calls

00601

cold winds blow
there is no shiver
when faking love and life

but there is a warm space between us
and a jar to keep sweets in

00603

the cloudless roof
was proof that I had crawled
several years
and trawled several fears
with a manmade map
mumbling with a mouthful of marbles
I spat and polished for kicks
and while sucking hell from leather
decided
like grapes on snow
to roll
singing....
as the urge to break glass
outweighs the urge to break bread
the urge to collapse
outweighs this need to be fed

00605

I was the part time job
for a soft summer
then rapid cells
touched a bowel
brought a lump to a throat
took a stool from a bar
and winter threw in a towel

00606

grace lays golden eggs
amongst the hardy hedgerow flowers
as custom adopts the wildlife
within the morning hours
our sun warms up the collage
of everything that grows
and points home the hammer
maneuvering where it blows
then evening darns home comforts
from sowing linear fields
and these horizons of a life
are reciprocal of the yields

00610

if I nod off
give me a nudge

if I stop breathing
don't hold a grudge

but always remember

a belfry of bats wasn't new
and a lion isn't king of a zoo

I so loved you xx

00613

such draining psychotic sleep
in such a harsh vengeful bed
focused on butterscotch
holding an involuntary shaking head

and there's an arse and an elbow
greeting chocolate with open legs
taking every drop of morality
from half a dozen eggs

throwing sticks to chewing bricks

it's a dog's life
it's a bleeding wife

on the rag with a big bag of tissues
whisking bulimic omelets
with revised immoral issues
turning it off turning it on
now she's here now she's gone

00614

when the devil bellows
wind and water mill
waking at the breaking
before the iron will
mother breaks the bread
as father time stands still
in field in hope in life
forever grow or kill

00615

on all fours
the flesh doth sway
pounded and punished
in a pious way
his knees were raw
from a meek disposition
so the priest taught him virtue
in the missionary position

00617

Individual personal responsibility
broke through my cellar door
with no eye contact nor manners
the canvas lay strewn on the floor
I've broken fingers
I've broken toes
I've broken my heart
and broken a nose
three times or thrice
it's still the price
and all because the birds and bees
are stirred with the sword of damocles
above my beloved art of violence

00618

my bleeding menstruation
was a bloody agitation
from a time of sanitation
to this hot and dry sensation

00619

looking at life to see what's what
I guess we're all the same
the price of what we have
the price of what we've not
and where to apportion the blame

00620

tapping on the window
of the genuine people's club
where brandy misplaces
and a big cigar embraces
all delectation is delayed
as pinafores harmonise
with the toll bells of steel
hanging bunting and bunting
on the latest big wheel
above industrial scale damsels
bringing bounty on their backs
laden with maiden
on treacherous old tracks
merely showboating
at their lack of meaningful invention

00621

some of the time
I'm a bag of organs
most of the time
tolerant
of the intolerant
and all this time
dreaming
of once upon a time

00624

another's will
Will tell
crying spell
the prize of death
riven pretend
love becomes fact
bastard nee friend
forlorn bad death
the good divorce
burn and bury
broken remorse

00625

brassy babble summer day
crescendo be done
bird song
be gone
squawking hawking dismay
pray bathe on harmonies of meadow
to celebrate our stone shadow
blackbirds unto this plot
bring peace on the wing
take bread for your king
for nature was never so
love me
love me not

00626

I have a wife
a house
a car
a dog
a job I hate
and an amazonian tree frog
whose name jack
and I lick his back
so that I forget
I have a wife
a house
a car
a dog
a job I hate
and an amazonian tree frog

00628

tears are our medals
when love is slain
but some never dry
nor ease the pain
tears are our medals
when joy is free
with pride in our hearts
for all to see
tears are our medals
when we say goodbye
thus the measure of life
are the tears that we cry

00629

my eyelids were eaten years ago
now my damaged dial
soaks in the cold sun
your brittle spittle
waxes lyrical upon my kindle skin
and for me
It's a fight to remain
sometimes a brief grief tussle
sometimes visions of heaven as hell
and for you
here's the church
here's the steeple

00631

my father was a bastard
and I'm a bastards son
thy kingdom come
thy will be done

00633

reflections of decree
there's more to life
than threepenny bits
and more to love
than sucking tits
but where the well wishes for water
predictable madness descends
incarceration holds liberation
and elementary darkness transcends
within
our universe
that's bigger than life
bigger than dreams
and the doorway at death
to abstract extremes

00636

I found a note
in a raincoat
on a sailboat
from a nanny goat
to a billygoat
she wrote
and I quote
don't dote or gloat
this in an anecdote

00637

I only kissed one of the Bronte sisters
irrespective of what they wrote
for attraction is purely physical
not some scrawl or graphic note
and on a whim I buggered Branwell
whilst he painted me in the nude
but he kept his socks on
to hold his brushes
after all I'm not a prude

00638

the distance
between hope and love
is fear
and the distance
between you and me
is here

00639

I've decided to be buried
in a shallow grave
in a big silk sack
like a tea bag
and without a predictable plaque
in the hard rains
I'll slowly add something good
back into the earth
for what it's worth
an unmanned fertile sainthood
or maybe if I'm lucky
I'll be dug up by a pack of wolves
under a full moon
a packed lunch with a starring role
or maybe I'll just stew
to a familiar morbid tune

00640

making full senseless
in and out of order
deaths door swings
a fat lady sings
on white hot coals
making full senseless
doffing my new face
begging changes nothing
and nothing of tomorrow
a silent heart of cool blood
a paperweight on sorrow
making full senseless
at the pure ugliness of me

00642

please don't fall in love with me
I hide the speechless dreaming
my love gets lost
within the stride
don't chide
it's somewhere gleaming
precious nothing's collide
my pride bows
at such bolide
and to those who've sighed
at this very meaning
my intension suffers crucified

00643

time
once upon a mantle piece
ticked all the boxes
and tocked the nicotine
for the football pools
are one thing
but so is tetrafleoroethalyne

00645

your shoes
walked close
on rain
and shine
to rest in peace
in front of mine

00646

alone
life takes me
to places
alone
it whispers
for better for worse
to enjoy
the perverse
alone
I look
and listen
with
a curse
somewhere between
alone
and atone